Mending the Heart You've Broken

A Man's Guide to Rebuild and Strengthen His Marriage

Maurice Martin

Mending the Heart You've Broken
Copyright © 2017 by Maurice Martin
ISBN: 978-0-9997999-1-8

Purpose Publishing
1503 Main Street #168
Grandview, Missouri 64030
www.PurposePublishing.com

Bulk Ordering Information:
Quantity sales. Special discounts are available on quantity purchases by churches, ministry associations, and others. For details, contact the publisher at the address above.

Author Inquiries:
Maurice.martin64@yahoo.com

Scriptures used in this book are from the King James Version and Amplified Versions of the Bible.

Printed in the United States of America.

PRAISES FOR MENDING THE HEART YOU'VE BROKEN

Pastor Martin and his wife have impacted our marriage in a number of ways. First and foremost, they are both incredible examples of being followers of Christ. Pastor Martin is a God-fearing and respectable leader of his home and exemplifies Paul's edification of an overseer in 1 Timothy 3. Mrs. Martin is a prayer warrior, strong believer, and an example for younger women to follow. Pastor and Mrs. Martin began impacting our marriage by being Christ-like leaders and examples to us while we were single. Upon our engagement, we were privileged to have Pastor Martin and his wife conduct our premarital counseling. They shared godly advice from time-tested principles they have walked out themselves. We were also afforded the opportunity to see how they addressed issues in a godly way within their family.

We were blessed to receive counsel and advice from them, after we were married, to help us walk through tough times and continue to strive to be better when times were good. One particular piece of advice given to us was to stick together like a pair of scissors. When anything tries to attack or come between a couple, through prayer, togetherness, and love, the attack can be stopped like a pair of scissors comes together to cut through paper. The Martins continue to be supportive of our marriage as they were from the beginning. It is so refreshing to see a couple who truly love and like each other. Receiving counsel and correction from them is always welcomed because they share truth in love and live out what they teach.

Love, Zack and Diana

Pastor and Mom Martin are truly a gift from God. They genuinely have the heart of a Father and a Mother. Their prayers, support, love and correction gave us a tangible example of a Godly marriage. Because they are a true man and woman of God, our spirit man was receptive to their guidance.

Pastor Martin gets how men operate and hears from the Holy Spirit. Mom Martin connects with the soul of a woman. What we love most about them is that they are completely sold out to God but are earthly good! They're not strange and spooky. They're real!

We are approaching our 10th year of marriage and they absolutely have a hand in our success.

It's a privilege and an honor to have them in our lives. We can't say enough about how awesome they are and the impact they've made on us!

Shannon and Magna

There are either too many words or not enough words to praise Pastor and First Lady Martin. Without their love for God, people, each other, and successful marriages, the transition to marriage for my wife and I would have been tumultuous. Four years later, we are still grateful for their dedication to teaching us about marriage every Thursday evening in the months leading up to our ceremony. Though Pastor and First Lady had to display tough, unbiased love when appropriate, their honesty and passion for happy and healthy new marriages prove that Godly pre-marital counseling is imperative for engaged couples.

Jason & Aimee Anderson

Minister and Mrs. Martin,

I call them one of the best couples I know, for so many reasons. Both individuals have always exemplified excellence, love, consistency, and endurance.

Minister Martin has always been that silent killer. When he opens his mouth, knowledge is on its way out so you need to listen. Whatever he says will always connect to the word of God. The Martins were our premarital counselors. The main question they asked us was, "Are you ready for the work?" They taught us that marriage is work but it will work if God is in it and we communicate. They not only taught us that in those classes but they showed that whenever we saw them.

Mrs. Martin is a firecracker and will do whatever is needed to protect her family. She taught us no matter what anyone says always protect your family. You deal with your children in private but you protect them in public. As a woman, Mrs. Martin (Mom as I called her) taught me how to be a lady. Watch that hem line and make sure you're not giving the gift away. She also taught me that less in anything is more and compliments you much more than extreme. I know that was right because my husband says less makeup is much more appealing to him than overkill. 5 years later, we are still in love.

We contribute the health of our marriage to them and other examples that we have been able to watch and gleam from. They are a remarkable couple and we love them dearly.

Chudney and J.

On behalf of myself and my wife we'd like to thank you and your wife for being such an integral part of our development as a couple and ultimately as husband and wife. We had so much to learn when it came to blending as a family and the tools you gave us has certainly helped make a difference. My wife still quotes some of the things you said in our premarital counseling sessions.

We are so honored to have you as the person to marry us. If it wasn't for you and your wife my wife and I may not be married today. God bless you and your wife and there are a lot of couples out there who need what you and your wife have to give, just as me and my wife have.

Eric & Daphne Orphey

Elder Martin and his wife spoke truth, over my wife and I, and they would both say "DONT YOU GIVE UP" although they were not perfect they exhibited the character of the "Father." And though I knew they were faced with church environmental and even issues themselves it was their graceful determination that kept me watching their every move. He displayed what a Godly Man and husband looked like. They were and are to this day my Godly heroes in which I will always honor. They are examples of radical stewardship that continues to push and press toward a higher calling. They have blessed me, our family, and our marriage. I believe if my wife and I were asked to name a couple that has impacted our lives greatly in which we would always be connected, it would be Maurice and Jean Martin. I believe that they were part of my God given plan.

Thank you for teaching me through conversations and your action that I'm more than what I see in the mirror. Through your journey you have taught me how to identify, practice, and implement Godly truths. I can say with them in my life I better understand God's will for my life. His grace has changed my life forever! Now, I am passionate about showing people the true gospel of grace. I'm blessed and honored to be connect to such and Awesome Couple. I'll follow them to end, because of the God they follow. Love you.

Steve & Stacey Jones

DEDICATION

I would like to dedicate this book first and foremost to the woman who ultimately inspired me to write Mending the Heart You've Broken, my love, my heart, my rib and my helper my wife, Mrs. M. Jean Martin. Thank you for not giving up on us when times were hard and not giving up on me when it seemed I didn't perhaps deserve it. Your dedication to our vows and to God and to me is what helped me begin the mending process of our love when it was broken. Love you to life.

I would also like to dedicate this to my father, Pastor George Martin who transitioned to his heavenly home this year prior to the completion of my book and my loving mother, Vedora Martin. Their love and marriage withstood the time and challenges of fifty-four years. Thank you for all your love and support even when you didn't know you were supporting me. Mom, I love you forever and always. And to my siblings: Irish, Greg, Gary and DeeAnn, thank you for staying close. Love you all.

And to my children that stood with me through the good and challenging times. God bless each of you for your faithfulness to family and honoring me as your father.

I dedicate this book to the many couples my wife and I were privileged to counsel over the years. I thank all of you that trusted and obeyed the instructions my wife and I gave to help strengthen and build your relationships. May God keep His unchanging hand upon each of your marriages.

Finally, to the great men and women of God that were placed in my life along the way, those of you I've served for years and practically given my life to support your visions. In return, you have impacted my life in many different ways, and I say thank you. The late Bishop Kenneth Beckwith of Believer's in Christ Tabernacle, Ozark, AL who allowed me at age sixteen to move in and live with him and be taught many things about ministry and life. To Bishop Robert & Mary Pope who wrapped their arms around me and ordained me and helped cultivate me as a young minister to grow into an Elder of their growing congregation of Church of Deliverance, Junction City, KS for sixteen years. To Bishop Steve & Donna Houpe who continued to help me develop my leadership role in the ministry as well as my leadership role in my family. Thank you for also noticing the call upon my life and allowing me to be used in that gifting to edify God's people for sixteen years at Harvest Church International Outreach, KC, MO. I would also like to extend a special thanks to Pastor Martin & Lanelle Williams for their encouragement, prayers and loving support. Love you both.

You may have noticed in my dedications I mentioned the number sixteen three times. This number has great significance in my life. As I began to pray and meditate on this one day, God spoke to me in reference to this number and pointed out to me that "16" is for me, the number of transition. Sixteen is a multiple of eight, which is the number for new beginnings. Sixteen being two times eight paints a picture to me of twice beginnings. If I missed the first beginning, I didn't start my new beginning until the second time around. Perhaps I forfeited a blessing by not transitioning sooner, but God always gives me a second chance to start again. I would lag in making transitions because I feared the ending of the present even if the present wasn't always good for me. In order to start something new, something old has to end. And we, by nature, resist change.

And so, I foremost dedicate this book to my Lord and King Jesus Christ for pushing me to change by ending one phase of my life in order for me and my wife to begin a new phase.

TABLE OF CONTENTS

INTRODUCTION

My name is Minister Maurice Martin. I believe it is destiny for me to be a voice for the marriage union and to impact the lives of many to be better men and women. I had the idea of this book quite a few years before I actually wrote it. I don't rush into much as you will find out about me. I didn't want to rush into writing this book because it was important that I give you the best I can give and allow God to fill in the gaps.

I have a great desire to help as many marriages as I can pick up broken pieces and find the glue to put them back together again. My wife and I have counseled many couples helping them uncover and minister healing to the pain in their marriage. We've also performed many pre-marital counseling sessions with a tremendous conviction from our own lack thereof prior to our marriage. We focus on exposing individual issues and then impart the tools each will need to deal with issues that may not change in the spouse they have chosen or believe God has given them. Of course, there are some issues an individual may choose not to tolerate. In either case, they are saved from a future divorce or a terribly troubled marriage.

Mending the Heart You've Broken was birthed out of my own relationship with my lovely wife of thirty-two plus years. Our union has yielded four beautiful children divinely blended together, two of which my wife had prior to our marriage. We currently have ten wonderful grandchildren with more to come, I'm sure. I am not an old man. I started early. It sounds peachy, doesn't it? But it hasn't all been peachy. I made some huge mistakes along the way, and you probably have too, or else you wouldn't be holding this book in your hands. Some of those mistakes I thought I wouldn't be able to recover from, but with the help of God and a determination to save my marriage and family, I stand to say I'm still here.

Chapter 1

IN THE BEGINNING

Everyone has a beginning. And it is important to know where I began to understand how I got where I am. I also believe it is important for you to know where you began in order to process why you are where you are.

I grew up in a small town in L.A. (Lower Alabama that is), Ozark, Alabama. I consider myself not to have had the worst life growing up, but it wasn't the best life either. I want to be careful not to hurt anyone in this book as I tell this story, a true story, therefore I may not get as detailed as I would perhaps like.

I began my childhood living in the country with pigs and chickens running around in the yard. A rooster's crow woke us up every morning. We lived in a house, a shack really, with basically two or three families. There was no such thing as having your own room. The house only had about three rooms' period, or I should say sections. We had a big black potbelly, wood burning stove to heat the home. I remember sleeping with my mother in the bed in the room with the heater. Sleep was so peaceful underneath those heavy, hand woven quilts. It was great being in one place with my mother, aunties, uncles and cousins. My father worked highway construction and was gone a lot. I don't remember him being around much prior to five years old.

After coming off the road and taking another job, my dad decided to move us to town. At five years old, I thought that was great. I saw this new place no one had lived in prior to us. It seemed new, but later I learned we had moved to what we know today, and even then, as the projects. My dad worked hard back then, but he played hard too, if you know what I mean. Monday through Friday, he gave the man, as they use to say, his time and worked hard at it. But the weekends were his to do whatever he wanted to do. Sad to say, that hardly ever included the family. Dad hung out with his buddy, the bottle. As I remember it, he would be drunk all weekend. It was funny how he could be drunk all weekend and back to work ready to give the man one hundred percent on Monday morning. Well, I don't know about one hundred percent, but he was there. He always brought home his pay so we could eat and have a roof over our head. Thankfully, we weren't in the projects long. With all the fighting and shooting, it was time to move. The police constantly harassed the community for its behavior and sometimes because they could. This was the deep south in the late sixties and early seventies.

My dad was able to get us on a program to get a brand-new house, literally down the hill from the projects. The house was so new there wasn't even any grass in the yard. This was probably the beginning of our trying to be a family together.

Even though we had moved out of a hostile community, the hostility followed. My dad still had to shake the anger of living in those surroundings. I can't imagine what it would have been like if we had stayed. My father's drinking habit continued, but my mother was a praying woman who chose to stay with her husband and fight for her marriage. I'm not saying she was perfect. She had her moments, but she was never hooked on any type of substance. And eventually, my dad turned his life around, gave up drinking and became a pastor of a small congregation in the small town of Opp, AL, for over twenty-five years before his transition to his heavenly home in January 2017.

This is a glimpse of who I am and where I come from, which is relevant because where you come from can affect your relationships tremendously.

My wife and I truly believe God himself put us together. Despite our differences, we're a match made in heaven. We gave into love shortly after her first marriage ended in a nasty divorce. I was a young man of twenty years, serving my country in the US Army and never before married, when I found myself with eyes for a young lady who was not what momma told me to look for in a wife, a divorcee with two children. Momma said, "Don't marry no woman with kids and stay away from women with other men's (baby daddy) issues because you might get killed!" Momma was trying to look out for me, and I can appreciate that. But here I was in love with this woman asking her to marry me and for the sake of love, she said yes.

In the beginning, marriage was great. We loved being around each other. Despite not starting out with much, we were hyped because we loved each other. We rented a small 550 square foot home right outside the army base until we could get housing on post. The house had about five rooms, six if you count the small, screened in back porch. There were two bedrooms with a shared bath in between, a kitchen and living room and lots of love in the place. I was trying to give the kids all the love of a stepfather who stepped in when their biological father stepped out, and my wife and I were giving each other all the love. It was a loving atmosphere. After a while, things started to surface, and because we hadn't given ourselves a heads up on these issues, we didn't always know how to handle them. We began to do things, sometimes even unknowingly, that hurt each other.

In this book, I don't want to focus on my hurt but rather the hurt I inflicted. As a man, I have learned you can't change anyone but yourself. For the benefit of those who think the principles in this book don't apply to you, let me reassure you, it does. I don't care if you verbally abused, cheated, neglected, or failed to financially secure your wife, it applies to you.

My days in the military often required me to be gone for a couple weeks, a month, six months and ultimately an entire year, separating me from my wife and kids. The reunion was always great, but unlike the adage, "absence makes the heart grow fonder," the days after the initial reunion were sometimes the toughest. The more I was away, the more I found myself living as a single man again. It's easy when you are absent not to be as affected by the emotional needs of the family as when you are there. Sometimes, because of where and how you were raised, it may be easy to distance yourself even though you are there. Let me assure you, because you are there physically does not mean you are there.

After I ended my days in the military, I was home every night, but soon started to travel with my new job. I worked many hours during the day and then became involved in ministry. I spent all my free time at the church allowing God to use me in many ways to effect change in our church. I was elevated to Elder and began to assist my pastor closely. If speed dial had existed then, my number would have most likely been the first one. Sadly, while I was ministering to the needs of the congregation, my family's needs were being neglected. This was no fault of the church. I take full responsibility for my oversight. I was given stewardship over my family, and I was not being a good steward. I wasn't totally neglecting them. I did love my family, and I knew there should have been more time given to them.

To resolve this, I implemented a family day. We had reached a point in our ministry where every night was taken except Thursday, so I took it. Come hell or high waters, nothing would interfere with our family night.

Money wasn't in abundance at the time, therefore we didn't do expensive things. We rode out to the lake and played in the park or went fishing. We did pizza and a video. Sometimes, we played Uno. I was in charge of coming up with our planned activity each week, but I also took suggestions.

Strange as this may sound, this wasn't doing much for building my relationship with my wife. It did help me gain greater respect for rallying the family and showing them they were important to me, but this wasn't the same as spending time with her. We are a blended family. We came into our relationship with our kids from day one. There was never a time for us to get to know each other without the kids. Understand this, I was not only building a relationship with my new wife, I was building one with my new children as well. I believe subconsciously I knew this was going on, but I don't believe I focused on this with purpose. Raising your children and not letting them raise themselves requires a lot of work and tireless time training and correcting them. Unfortunately, this meant my wife was getting what was left over after work, church and kids, which wasn't much, and it wasn't fair to her at all.

After years of this, I purposed in my heart to do something to fix this. The kids were getting older, and I felt I could trust them with someone while my wife and I took some time away together. The first time we got away was like a breath of fresh air. Our first day alone, we tried to enjoy each other's company but wondered what was going on with the kids. We called and checked in, which allowed us to concentrate on each other. The two days alone did wonders for our relationship. Before we returned to our normal routine, I purposed to do a getaway every two or three months as funds allowed. However, the getaways soon fizzled and before we knew it, we weren't going any more. Vacation became driving once a year with the kids to my hometown or hers.

The most primary relationship in the family is your relationship with your spouse.

Later, we were blessed to take trips with the kids to see other parts of the country, and we loved it. I love spending time with my family, always have. But again, there was distance between my wife and me. It's important to remember, the most primary relationship in the family is your relationship with your spouse.

I eventually realized my relationship with my wife had more of an impact on my children than my actual relationship with them. Children become what they see in their home. If you are not taking the time to build a relationship with their mother, you are tearing down the relationship you are trying to build with your kids.

My wife tried to tell me our relationship was breaking down, but I wasn't listening…at least not with my heart.

Chapter 2

LISTENING TO THE HEART

Most men, and I was no different, tend to hear the words coming out of their wife's mouth, but taking time to listen is a whole new arena. I find most men, even when talking to each other, simply listen to the highlights and then respond instead

> **Men tend to listen to the highlights and then respond.**

of evaluating all the words, the presentation of the words, and the atmosphere in which the words are presented to them. My wife would always say, "You're not listening to me!" And my reply would be, "Yes, dear. I heard you!" Hearing and listening can often be two different things. We were not effectively communicating. Men tend to listen to the highlights and then respond

Over the years, our marriage experienced some serious bumps in the road. Finances were never the best, but we made do with what we had. Because of where we both came from, not having a lot wasn't a big issue. Our credit was pretty good so getting credit cards wasn't a problem…or, maybe it was a problem. We bought a new car off the showroom floor. With me being in the military, we were able to get into on-post housing, which meant we had no mortgage or utility expenses except cable. We were living in the time of life when credit was the best way to buy things. We acquired a significant amount of debt that we made payments on each month. If only we knew back then what we know now. We were headed for the old debt trap. And, man did it get us. I was never taught anything about debt management or how to budget finances. I had to learn the hard way. I thought as long as I could afford to make the payments, I should charge up those credit cards until I couldn't make the payments. And I had been leading my wife down this road for a while.

I remember purchasing a new bedroom suite for our new house on base. I wanted to impress her with a grand bedroom set. She said to me, "I don't think we should get this set right now. It seems like a lot of money." And I said, "The salesman says it will only be so many dollars a month." It was a grand high-rise waterbed with the big post and mirrors in the top.

She told me more than once not to make the purchase. "I don't need a waterbed," she said, "I'm fine with a regular bed." I heard her, but I wasn't listening to her. I was determined to get that bed, so I could work my magic as Charlie Wilson said.

Had I paused to listen to my wife's heart, I would have learned she didn't like waterbeds and the security of not having an extra payment meant more to her than being impressed.

I bought the bed on credit and later found out she hated the bed, and my magic wasn't working well enough for her to get over her dislikes of this bed. She said, "I tried to tell you, but you wouldn't listen!" I tried to negotiate with the company we bought the bed from to give it back and get another set, but the company said all sales were final.

Not listening to the heart of your wife can lead you into things that can't be changed. Never make a decision without deep consideration of your wife's input. Though you may be the final decision

The little things a woman may say to us if we listen with the intent to hear her heart will give us all we need to make her life happy and fulfilling.

maker, it doesn't mean you are the sole decision maker.

After going around and around with the company, they modified the bed, conformed it to a regular bed and sold me an expensive mattress on top of what I already paid. I was young and dumb. But, I should have learned two lessons that day, one about finances and the other about listening to my wife's heart. This was the beginning of me hearing and not listening to my wife.

Often, my wife made comments about things she needed or expressed a desire to talk about this or that. Caught up in working, stressing over bills, kids and trying to be available for God to use me in ministry, I would nod and say, "Okay, I hear you," telling her I understood something, when my actions displayed the complete opposite.

The little things a woman may say to us if we listen with the intent to hear her heart will give us all we need to make her life happy and fulfilling. When she says, "I need to go to the mall to look at some shoes," but doesn't make an effort to head out the door, she may actually be saying, "I would like for us to spend some time together today." She may not even buy shoes, but she's trying to buy some time with you.

Men aren't great listeners, by nature. We often listen with a motive to hear what the problem is so we can fix it and be on our way. The word of God says, "No man knows the

> ***The hearing of the heart must be practiced with the intent of getting to know what's in the heart of our spouses.***

heart but God." But the Word of the Lord also says, "Out of the heart does the mouth speak," which leads me to believe though the heart is not known by us initially, as it is with God, we can hear or gain access to the heart through the words that come from our spouses' mouth. The hearing of the heart must be practiced with the intent of getting to know what's in the heart of our spouses.

Imagine that!

Chapter 3

ASSESSING THE DAMAGE

Listening to the heart allows you to assess the damages. This is perhaps the biggest step to recovering from a major hurt. It's also the most difficult to do. If we avoid talking about the issue, we will circumvent the mending process.

> **If you neglect to assess the small damages in your relationship, you will face a much greater cost to repair the larger damages.**

After a serious car accident, the first thing we do is assess the damages created by the collision. But when the accident isn't major, like hitting a small pothole in the road, we hardly ever stop to assess the damages. We keep on driving. Relationships experience accidents all the time. And it seems, more times than not, we never take the time to assess the damages before trying to move on. I believe it was Bishop TD Jakes who said we sometimes run over potholes in our life and keep on going all the time. Then, we hit a big one and it forces us to finally pull over and assess the damages. But now, we're dealing with all the damage from every pothole we've hit up to this point. My friend, if you don't take the time to address the small issues, the ones you don't think warrant your attention, you will soon hit a huge pothole and that one collision will

> *Neglecting problems don't make them go away. Sorry.*

force you to stop and recognize the severe damage in your relationship. Whether you are busy following a career or ignorant of the things you're doing to hurt your companion, you will have to stop and address the damages you have inflicted. If you neglect to assess the small damages in your relationship, you will face a much greater cost to repair the larger damages.

Neglecting problems don't make them go away. Sorry. I can't begin to tell you how many times I ignored the problems my wife and I were having, hoping they would go away. They never did. Even if you avoid hitting any potholes for a while and laughter abounds, and you appear to be having a good time, the pothole you hit months ago is still hurting your relationship.

Recently, I was driving my car and heard a small noise, one I had heard many other times. Because the car had stopped making the noise for a while, I thought it was fine. I drove the car all day long without any problems, got home, pulled into the garage and entered the house. Later, when I went back out, the noise was louder and much more noticeable. I waited for the car to quiet down and shifted to reverse but nothing happened. I shifted to drive and guess what? Nothing happened. All of a sudden, my transmission was gone. But it wasn't all of a sudden. The signs had been there for a while. I wasn't listening attentively enough to act. The price I now had to pay to get my car back on the road was pretty heavy. But I paid it, and it's rolling fine. Listening with your heart will produce your willingness to change.

> ***Listening with your heart will produce your willingness to change.***

The same is true of our relationships. We journey along not listening to the noises in our relationships. We hear the noise, wait for it to quiet down, and think we can keep on rolling. Sooner or later, a major shut down happens and like my car, we can't go backward, and we certainly can't go forward until the damages have been repaired. Go ahead. Settle it with yourself right now. There is going to be a huge price to pay to get this relationship back on the road. Man up and pay the price! You have to be willing to hear with your heart what you haven't wanted to hear all this time with your ears. Listening with your heart will produce your willingness to change.

While you are listening, remember that men and women are different, even in the way they communicate.

Chapter 4

KNOWING YOUR DIFFERENCES

There is no way to approach healing a woman's hurts without first understanding that she is not you. Even in every day relations with people in general, we often forget everyone doesn't think like us or function the way we do. We tend to say things and respond to others based on who we are versus who the person we are dealing with is. I know it is impossible to know everyone we deal with in such a way as to always be absolute in every circumstance, but we are talking about the woman or man you say you love. Men and women are different. But in some ways, they are the same. Remember God didn't create woman from the dust of the ground as he did man. He created woman from man. So, there must be a little bit of man in woman and then less of women in men, if any. I believe because women have been equipped with part of men, it is sometimes easier for women to understand men than it is for men to understand women. Men struggle so hard to understand women. Perhaps because men weren't created from the inward part of women. This means it won't come naturally for men to know women. We have to intentionally learn who women are.

Woman

The scriptures tell men, "… husbands dwell with them (wives) according to knowledge…" (1Peter 3:7). Men have to study women and open their minds to be taught who the woman is, how she's made and what her purpose is. The Bible says God removed one of Adam's ribs to form woman.

In order to get the kind of woman God has for man, it has always required a sacrifice of part of himself.

The ribs work as pairs to protect and support other vital organs of the body. When God said it's not good for man to be alone, He perhaps was saying we shouldn't be without our support, which we can truly find in our helpmate, our wives, or as some say, our rib. The one major organ of the body protected by the rib is the heart. Perhaps there is some correlation as to why God chose to form woman out of a part of man's body designed to protect the heart. I believe we have to learn to remove the hard covers we use to protect our manliness to give the woman access to our hearts. Women are built to carry or nurture. Once she conceives and a seed is planted in her womb, she will carry or nurture the seed until it is birthed. It's the same for women spiritually and emotionally as it is physically. Not only do we plant seeds of children in our wives, we also plant other seeds.

We give them things to carry and nurture until something is birthed. When I came to grips with the fact that I planted the seed I was reaping in my wife, it blew my mind. I argued with God and myself. There was no way I caused her to treat me the way she treated me. No way!

I was wrong.

We will reap the birth of every seed we've sown into our relationship. As a young soldier in the early stages of our marriage, the military taught me, "Duty first." But, where did that put my wife? She was running a close

> *We will reap the birth of every seed we've sown into our relationship.*

second, but I could get so wrapped up in the first, there was a vast distance to get to second. Not only did I have the military telling me duty first, I was also involved in my church. Church teaches us, "God first," which is often interpreted as "church first." For the record, God and the church are not the same. I believe I should always keep God first. This means as the scriptures says in Matthew to seek first the kingdom of God and His righteousness and all the things will be added by

Him. With two of my obligations warring to be first in my life, the best my wife could get was a good third place. And there were the children! We had children from the beginning of our union. I had to make them feel as important as my wife was to win their love. For years, I was unaware of what I was sowing into my relationship with my wife.

Now I realize I was sowing seeds of:

- You are not as important as my job.

- You are not as important as the church.

- You are as important as the children, but not more so.

- You are (in her words) on the back burner.

I came home tired and gave her my leftovers, which wasn't much. I missed most of our conversations trying not to fall asleep. My wife carried this until she couldn't carry it any more. And then, the baby (the seed I planted) was birthed, with all of the tone, elevations, tears and emotions you could imagine. And I responded in the stupidest way I could. "What did I do?"

Often, we are tempted to defend ourselves and find fault in our spouse to cover up our faults. Don't! She's not going to kill you, yet. She wants you to hear her. And because we didn't hear her when she spoke nicely, now we have forced her to speak out like a man, because that's the only way she thinks she can get her point across.

In the Bible, God calls the woman the weaker vessel, which doesn't mean there aren't some women out there who can whip a man. God forbid! Yet, if something is weaker, you have to take better care of it and pay closer attention to it in hopes of protecting it from being broken. If the woman is the weaker vessel, this means we are the opposite, the stronger vessel. Regardless of how much she is spouting off about all you haven't done, it doesn't change how God made you. Take your

> ***Hurt doesn't just go away with time.***

feelings off your shoulders, drop your pride and listen with the intent to change. We know the truth when we hear it, and sometimes it doesn't feel good. But it's all part of paying the price for not doing proper maintenance earlier.

I wish I could say I was the perfect example, but I was still hanging on to my pride. I felt like I was being attacked. When we feel attacked, we set up defenses: shut down, yell back, walk out or deny everything as if our spouse is crazy. I was so thrown off by her allegations, I shut down and didn't say anything. However noble that may seem, I also wasn't discussing the problem. I was silently fighting on the inside and not taking responsibility for planting the seed in the first place. My wife gave birth to lowered self-esteem, insignificance, and insecurity. I would never "knowingly" inflict this kind of hardship on my wife. And I pray you haven't either. If you have, it's not too late with God's help to change, especially if you haven't lost your spouse already.

Hurt doesn't just go away with time. I know the old saying, "Everything heals with time" or "time heals all wounds." As

> **God is not obligated to fix what you've broken, but He will help you put the pieces back together if you ask Him.**

one of my former pastors would say, "That's a bunch of bunk!" The crying may stop after a while, the tears may dry for a while and the talk may stop for a while, but only until something happens to reveal the wound is still there. Most of us, men and women, walk around with suppressed hurts that have never been confronted or dealt with. Clear your mind now of thinking the problem will go away if you wait long enough, that they will be okay with a little time. No, No, No! It doesn't work like that.

Another avoidance tactic is to say, "Let's pray about it. God will take away the hurt and fix our relationship." Lest you forget, we are the ones who planted the seed of hurt. It isn't fair to ask God to fix it.

God is not obligated to fix what you've broken, but He will help you put the pieces back together if you ask Him. In all your ways acknowledge Him and He will direct your path. (Prov. 3:6) We must always consider God in our actions to get a much clearer path to the process. It will also help us to avoid some of the delays that we cause ourselves in the process. THE HUSBANDMAN

"I am the true vine, and my Father is the husbandman" *(John 15:1).*

In the scriptures, Jesus speaks of Himself being the vine and God the Father being the husbandman. This intrigued me to study husbandman. He didn't say husband, but husbandman. The husbandman was the tender or cultivator of the grounds. Without distorting the text, I conclude husband, as the base word, compares to husbandman (one who cultivates). This leads me to believe the husband is to cultivate his God given responsibilities, including his wife, as a farmer does his grounds to plant new seeds. The ground has to be readied to receive the seeds. We can't plant seeds until the ground has been prepared to receive it. Likewise, we can't plant what we expect to grow in our wives until we have prepared her for those seeds. Just as there are seasons for planting certain vegetables, there are appropriate times to plant thoughts or new decisions about where you and your family are headed. You can't start teaching your spouse lessons of life or scriptures from God's word after hurt has been inflicted

> *The setup is as important as the delivery. There has to be cultivation before planting.*

on her. Her ground isn't ready for those seeds. This is often where we attempt to get our point across about how we've been treated. "Let me be blunt," we say. No sir, this is not the time to flaunt your ego or your feelings at all. I believe you can pretty much say whatever you need to say to a person if it's said with tact. The way you say something is as important as, maybe even more important than, what you say.

The setup is as important as the delivery. There has to be cultivation before planting. Every farmer (husbandman) knows cultivating the ground is perhaps the hardest part of the harvest process, especially if the ground has been sitting unattended for a while. Rugged terrain must be tilled, which includes turning over the ground so you can get to what is underneath, because the soil underneath is the good soil. I had to realize the soil of my wife had been sitting unattended for a while, and it was up to me to deal with all the weeds that had grown where perhaps vegetables or flowers could have been planted. When I looked at the task ahead, it was so much

> *If we aren't willing to dig a little and deal with the hard stuff, it will be impossible to plant.*

easier to sit back and hope it would somehow work out with time. But the only thing time would do is give way to more weeds and firm up the ground even more, making it that much harder to turn over. If we aren't willing to dig a little and deal with the hard stuff, it will be impossible to plant.

Ask your wife the tough questions and then be willing to accept what she says. If this is the first time you've heard what she is saying, or you think this is the first time you've heard this, tell her. She might say, "This is not the first time I told you this," or, "You don't ever listen to me!" Fess up and tell her she is absolutely right, but you are ready to listen with your heart with the intent to hear and truly make a conscious effort to change. And please make sure you have prayed before you do this. Ask God to help you mean what you say. As men, whatever we put our minds to do, we normally do, even if it's wrong. Am I right?

Sometimes, it takes a while to dig up all the old stuff that has been planted because the roots have been there for so long.

If you've been making promises you never keep, it's time to get it together. How do you fix what's over when you can't go back? Begin to make promises you CAN keep on a regular. Start with small things like, "I promise I will take the trash out at eight o'clock, and do it, not at a minute later. I don't care if you have to use your cell phone as a reminder or set an alarm clock or stick a post it note on your forehead. Come hell or high water, get it done when you say it's going to be done. Promise to put gas in the car and do it. If you say you'll take care of getting the kids to bed, do it when you say you'll do it. It doesn't take you bringing home a million dollars to regain her trust. The more you do the little things you promise, the more your words will mean something again. And your words will also start to mean more to you as well. Stop making promises you can't keep. This is all a part of tilling the ground so you can plant new seeds.

> *I called on God, my heavenly father, my deliverer and restorer and asked for help.*

Sometimes, it takes a while to dig up all the old stuff that has been planted because the roots have been there for so long. There had been years of old roots I hadn't taken the time to dig up. In some instances, I had watered the old roots and caused them to go deeper. At the time we were going through all this stuff, I didn't realize what I was doing. I thought a simple "I'm sorry" would be good, and we should be able to move on. Nope! Not even my sincere heartfelt "I'm sorry," the one where I meant every word of my apology and intended to never go down that road again fixed our issues. It had taken me years to do this damage, I certainly couldn't fix it all in one day. I called on God, my heavenly father, my deliverer and restorer and asked for help. I asked Him repeatedly to fix the hurt in my wife. "Surely if you are the creator of all things, you can heal this hurt in my wife," I prayed. And I'll never forget his response. He said, "I didn't do this to her. You did, and you have to fix it."

Don't expect God to fix what you've broken!

I felt like a ton of bricks dropped on me. "What?" I asked God in a state of awe. He repeated it back to me again, like I didn't hear it the first time. "Man, I can't fix this!" I said to God in a voice of panic. But God has a way of calming me down when I get all worked up. I continued to pray and study His word. Then God reminded me of many occasions where He placed the responsibility back on us to receive the things we request from him. One scripture came to mind, (Deuteronomy 8:18) the part that says, "It is He that gives us the power to get wealth." God doesn't drop wealth on us because we pray for it but He does give us the

> *God will be our help in the moment when we are in our time of trouble.*

power or the authority to change our present state. God was letting me know that I have been given the power to get one of the most valuable things in my life back. What greater wealth is there than to have a marriage made whole? And then I was also encouraged by Psalms 46:1 "God is our refuge and strength, a very present help in trouble."

God will be our help in the moment help when we are in our time of trouble.

God is our refuge and strength, a very present help in trouble (Psalms 46:1).

God will be our help in the moment when we are in our time of trouble. He will be the HELP! And if I was ever in trouble, I was definitely in trouble at that point in our marriage. I accepted that if our marriage was going to continue, it was up to me with the help of God to mend what I had broken.

Chapter 5

CLEAVING

Therefore shall a man leave his father and his mother, and shall cleave unto his wife: and they shall be one flesh (Genesis 2:24).

When times get tough in relationships, it's always easier to walk away. If there's one thing I learned from watching my parents go through rough spells in their marriage, it's not to throw in the towel. There were a number of occasions where they were packed and ready to give up on each other, but a conversation always somehow upended the departure.

"Nothing in a relationship keeps it stronger than cleaving. Not words. Not holding hands. Not even sex." Bishop Steve Houpe

Cleaving is not letting go even when trouble comes. It is holding on to something as if your life depended on it. One thing that builds a relationship like nothing else is sticking together in troubled times. There ought to be a great sense of love and appreciation for a person you know had all the rights in the world to leave you but chose to stay.

"No one has to stay with you, they do have the option to leave! But the mere fact they are still there is a sign they want to be with you." Bishop Steve Houpe

Most people hang on to a relationship until things aren't working the way they think it should or better yet, not working for their benefit. We don't always realize it, but our nature is to take care of *numero uno*. Society has taught us that no one is going to take care of you but you. We develop selfish attitudes that tend to carry over into our relationship with our spouse. This is not the way it should be. Here's the question. When we get married, are we marrying to be loved or to give love? It should be the latter. You reap what you sow. You can only get out of a relationship what you put into the relationship. It will be heaven on earth when two people are doing all they can to out-love each other. True love always, always gives. Love never fails. It always forgives.

Years ago, Bishop Steve Houpe mentioned in one of his messages five things to catch a drowning marriage:

1. The art of knowing
2. The art of listening
3. The art of waiting
4. The art of forgiving
5. The art of openness

Although he didn't go into great detail on these five things, I developed my own understanding through deep thought and study.

1. *Knowing:* The old saying, "What you don't know won't hurt you" is a lie. Not knowing what the issues are or being ignorant of your wife's/husband's needs will tear your marriage up. It may be a slow death, but eventually it will die. Find out what she or he needs from you. Couples go years thinking they're hitting on all cylinders while missing all or some.

Knowledge is indeed Power...When applied Correctly.

The power you gain from knowledge in your relationship is the power to change your relationship. You can't

> ***Knowledge is indeed Power...When applied Correctly.***

change what you have no knowledge of. In school, knowledge is gained by studying. Some subjects are harder for some of us to understand. Thus, it takes much more intense study time to absorb this particular level of knowledge. Marriage is a life-long school of learning. No one has all the answers and if they say they do, it is likely they need to study a little deeper. There are so many different circumstances and different types of people, it seems there is no formula for making our relationships smooth sailing down a non-rippling river. Many obstacles we face in our lives are mostly unexpected ripples and in some cases tides. However, with proper knowledge of your spouse and your current and past situations, you can govern your actions in a way that can aid in mending a broken heart.

You have to purposely determine to know everything you can to help heal the wounds you've inflicted. Study them as if a huge test follows. Truth be told, there is! And you will pass the test based on how well you've studied.

2. *Listening:* You cannot know without listening. As I previously said, listening is not the same as hearing. Hearing doesn't require action, but listening does. When you listen, you should be listening with both your ears and your heart. Anytime something gets in our heart, we tend to act on it. Knowledge in and of itself has no value unless it is packed into a heart that is on fire. You're not listening if at the same time your spouse is talking you're conjuring up what your response is going to be or what your next accusation will be. That's probably what caused the wreck in the first place. Listen with the intent of placing yourself in their shoes for the moment and try to experience what it is they're saying to you.

This will create one of the most intimate moments in your relationship, guaranteed. Learn how to cut out distractions like the television, radio or the kids. These moments demand a dedicated portion of undivided attention. Clear your heart of as much of your day as possible. You can go back and pick up stuff after the conversation. Believe me, it's not going anywhere. It will be right there waiting on you when you finish.

3.   *Waiting:*

One of the greatest tests to pass in life is the test of time. You've said your "I'm sorry" and you've started to change some things to become better.

> *I found out sometimes, it doesn't take words to say what the heart is speaking.*

You're even manning-up to your word, but it seems like they don't notice the change. As a matter of fact, they still bring up what you did every opportunity they get. Maybe it's been a week, a month, four months or longer, and every now and then you still hear, "You did such and such to me." You are faced with the challenge of waiting for them to acknowledge the change, recognize it and even show some appreciation for it. If you are making the proper adjustments, they notice the effort. But they aren't comfortable enough to let you know you are doing well, because they're afraid you might revert back to the old you. You're waiting on them to acknowledge you've changed, and you will be tempted to lash out and point out what you've done to change and all the progress you've made, but don't. I can't tell you I didn't make this mistake once or twice or a number of times. I also noticed when I did this, it set me back a little, and I lost some ground I had covered.

I found out sometimes, it doesn't take words to say what the heart is speaking. While you wait, pray and talk to God about the things you've changed and ask Him to work on their heart while you are working on yours.

4. *Forgiveness:* I almost skipped this one since I've been speaking from the position of needing to be forgiven. Over the course of me breaking my wife's heart, it caused her to lash out at me, and I found myself holding things against her and becoming bitter. I felt justified because I felt like she was hurting me too. That mindset leads to a game of tit for tat. "You don't forgive me, I don't forgive you either!" In my situation, and perhaps yours, I had to forgive first before I could move on to mending the other person.

"Hurting people; hurt people."

And when ye stand praying, forgive, if ye have ought against any: your Father also which is in heaven may forgive you your trespasses (Mark 11:25).

> ***Forgiveness is paramount in any relationship destined to grow.***

The Word of God tells us when we come to God in prayer the first thing we must do is forgive. It's the prerequisite to God having a conversation with us. I prayed often to God to help me, but until I got victory over my hurt and allowed myself to forgive my wife, I wasn't making any progress. I had to forgive her to stop bleeding on her, so I could see whose blood I was cleaning up, hers or mine (figuratively speaking).

Forgiveness is paramount in any relationship destined to grow. You've perhaps heard forgiveness is not for the person you forgive, it's for you. Holding on to unforgiveness may make us feel as if we are inflicting some kind of pain on the person we're not forgiving, but the truth is we damage ourselves in the process continuing to give life to the hurt done to us rather than killing it and moving on.

5. Openness: For men, being open isn't always the easiest thing to do. We live and work in environments built on being strong and not letting anyone see our weakness. We hide what's going on, finding it difficult to let others into our world. This also spills over into our relationships, but nothing can be resolved without trust. Refusing to be open and transparent with each other becomes a wall that prevents mending any hurts a relationship has experienced.

I went to the store one day and arrived a little late. How did I know I was too late? The sign on the door said closed, which meant there weren't going to be any

> *The unwillingness to be open is unfair to the person who shares their feelings openly.*

transaction between the merchant and me. The door was locked, and the lights were turned off. Because they were closed, I couldn't even look at what was available to purchase. Our relationships can also be this way. When one of us has put up the closed sign and we're not willing to open for dialogue and to express our feelings, there can be no transactions to heal each other. If we're not open, the other person can't even see what's available to deal with.

I have always been a kind of quiet non-confrontational person unless the situation called for a different response. Because I didn't care to be talkative, it was easy for me to shut down when things weren't going well between my wife and me. After a while, she would come around and it would be okay, or so I thought. I didn't realize for my wife to be open about what she was feeling and me not being open was unfair to her.

> **Openness creates a platform for trust.**

The unwillingness to be open is unfair to the person who shares their feelings openly. Openness creates a platform for trust.

One of the greatest elements of any relationship is trust. Matter of fact, trust is the foundational element upon which all other elements are built. If you don't have this critical element, everything else is a lie. In moments of intense discussions, my wife often told me, "You sit there like you don't care about what I'm saying. Don't you have something to say?" My response would be, "You can't handle what I have to say!" I would walk off and not ever get into it again. She told me she didn't know if she could trust me because we only discussed what she was dealing with, but I shielded her from what I was dealing with. And believe me, I was dealing with things as well.

I believe my inability or unwillingness to open up to my wife about my issues stemmed from not seeing my father talk to my mother about any of his issues. I don't blame him. Back in those days, the men I was around kept their feelings and their issues from their family. Perhaps this came from the idea of protecting the family from information husbands felt the family should be sheltered from. I honestly thought I was doing my wife a favor by not sharing my issues, feelings and gripes. I was not thinking about losing her trust. Anytime there is an unfair trade of information or if one spouse is open and the other is not, it will open the door to a lack of trust.

If you've created the hurt and you don't want to deal with it, then you're creating another wound that will need mending down the road. Avoiding the issue isn't going to make it go away. Perhaps you're thinking your spouse will forget about it if you don't deal with it, but women like to know you have a voice in a dispute. Oftentimes, your willingness to be transparent with your wife will begin the healing process. Whether they like it or not, they still want to hear what you have to say from your heart. Even women who like to be in control will eventually devalue you if you let them stay in control and do all the talking. Why? You ask. Because women want to feel secure, and she will take your lack of expression as a weakness, thereby feeling unprotected.

Chapter 6

Feeling the Pain

I'm not trying to convey that love is based on a feeling, but pain is definitely a feeling. Our emotions are feelings we experience internally. Most of us have heard or even been told, "Put yourself in the other person's shoes." It's easier said than done. But if we can make ourselves feel the pain of another, we can

> *Even though we try to envision being someone else, we still are not them.*

better help each other with the healing process. Of course, if we were experts at this, we may have never hurt them in the first place. It would be so amazing to actually change, literally change places with your spouse like in the movie, *The Change Up*. If we could do this with our wives or husbands, we would have a serious awakening. Even though we try to envision being someone else, we are not them. Though we should try to feel others' pain as much as possible in order to identify with what they are going through, to tell your spouse, "I know what you're feeling," may not be the best path toward healing.

Even though we try to envision being someone else, we still are not them. Everyone in this world, at some point in their life, has experienced pain or hurt. The best way perhaps for you to feel someone else's pain is to equate it with something that has hurt you. If your spouse tells you you've hurt them in a way words can't express, think about what you've felt so hurt by that you couldn't find words to express.

I once smashed my finger in the door of our home with such serious force that it almost fractured. I suffered a severe

Serious pain demands your attention!

blood clot in my fingernail leading to the loss of the nail, and I can't even begin to express the excruciating pain I felt at the onslaught of the injury. The pain was relentless.

Hopefully you're not physically hurting anyone, but can you imagine feeling this type of pain for days, weeks, months or even years? There are some emotional pains in our lives that feel this excruciating. And because we've felt this intense pain for so long, we tend to disconnect from any good feelings suppressed by the pain. Pain has a way of not allowing you to enjoy life. I know there are times when pain is good to push us into the direction of our destiny, but keeping the pain will destroy our chances of reaching our destiny. In feeling another's pain, you have to realize why it's so hard for you to get through to them. Yes, you said you were sorry. Yes, you said you wouldn't ever do it again. Yes, you said you would make it up to them. Yes, you said you would fix it. But bear in mind, when you're in serious pain, you don't want to hear anything. You want the pain to stop!

When I felt the pain in my finger, I didn't want to hear anybody's voice, nor did I want to be touched. The pain was so intense, I lost focus on what I was getting ready to do. I tried to take my mind off the pain, but the pain kept demanding my attention. That's what you're up against, my friend. Are you feeling the pain yet?

Serious pain demands your attention! There are times when pain will subside for a moment but it's still there until total healing takes place. Just because we can function by masking the pain or trying to suppress it for the sake of those around us, doesn't mean the pain has went away. The pain is still there, and it will continue to rear its head. I heard someone say pain has to have a place to lay its head. Pain needs a place to rest, and wherever it can find a comfortable place to lay its head is also a place where it can always raise its head. We've got to get better at kicking pain out and not giving it a place to reside in our hearts. It's important for couples to heal each other and not let pain linger. Whatever you've done to inflict pain in another, go to them and put your portion of healing oil on the wound to help them get over the hurt.

When a person has been hurt, they go through different stages: shock, numbness, physical and emotional pain. Physical pain can subside over time, while emotional hurt may remain long after the physical pain is gone.

Shock Hurt:

Shock hurt is the place where one disbelieves this is actually happening. What's happened is completely against the norm of what was expected when they married their spouse. This phase may include denial. You want to believe this is all a bad dream instead of reality. You remember all the things that brought you both goose bumps when you thought about each other. You reminisce about nights spent on the phone for hours before you got married, waiting for the other person to hang up before you did. Sometimes you fell asleep on the phone and woke up saying, "You still there?" If this is the way things began, then you are wondering, "What happened to that person?"

When a person experiences a tragic car accident, they often experience shock. They act as if things are okay while bleeding profusely or their leg is hanging off, unaware of their pain. It's as if the body refuses to react to tragedy. Perhaps you know you've inflicted pain upon a person, but they're not reacting as they should. They're in shock, and it hasn't hit them. When it does, you will know by their reaction to what has happened. I'm reminded of some Army veterans who were shot in battle. They said they didn't even know they were hit until someone else pointed it out. It's amazing how people who have been hurt can go years and not even know they've been hurt until they hear it from someone on the outside looking in.

> **The reality is nothing wrong can be revealed in a relationship if there's nothing wrong to be revealed.**

I remember the first time my wife expressed what she was learning about herself from books she was reading or conferences she attended. I was resistant. I thought she was letting those books tell her what was wrong with our marriage. I accused her of seeing things that were not there. But, the reality is nothing can be revealed in a relationship if it's not there. The only way a hurt person will ever heal is if they reach out and learn how to heal.

It's almost impossible to heal one's self by yourself. The less than enthusiastic response to the insights my wife shared with me were more about my neglect of personal responsibility to her than what she was learning about herself.

The reality is nothing wrong can be revealed in a relationship if there's nothing wrong to be revealed. One of the ways I helped heal the wounds I inflicted was to not minimize her feelings to make me feel better about myself. I had to give my wife the right to reach out for the aids she needed to help us heal the wound I had created. It will be difficult, if not impossible to mend another's broken heart when you're broken, hurting and needing to be mended yourself. I believe one of the ways to putting someone on the road to recovery is for them to see you taking the steps to put yourself on the road to recovery. My wife took that step by reaching out to a Christian counselor. If I choose not to take the steps she's already taken, I send a strong signal to her that I'm not willing to lay down my pride and step out of my comfort zone to do whatever it takes to help fix the damage I helped create.

There's no room for pride in this process. If you love your wife or husband (ladies), then you will act. We often say love is more than a word. Love is an action. And sometimes our actions are so different from the words we say. Saying we love and showing we love seems to be a reach for individuals who were not raised with a demonstration of love. We as are prone to follow what we see more so than what we hear. We have to change. We have to learn to do some things we are told even if we didn't see those things being modeled for us growing up. There are books filled with facts for life, and if we read or hear with the intent to give a

> *You have to learn to load your quiver with all the arrows you can to shoot for the target of making your relationship whole again.*

sincere effort to change then we can and will. Read the books, listen to the CD's or podcasts, watch the videos and attend the seminars. If you want to mend a relationship, you have to be willing to reach out for help. Information is so much easier to acquire today than it was twenty to thirty years ago. You've got to learn to load your quiver with all the arrows you can shoot to make your relationship whole again. I wasn't aggressive about making counseling happen. I procrastinated and dragged my feet. But when you want a change and you're tired of not enjoying all the moments you share with your spouse, you will get going and make it happen.

You have to learn to load your quiver with all the arrows you can to shoot for the target of making your relationship whole again. When you have finally allowed yourself to feel the pain, you will begin to shed a few tears as you carry the burden of guilt for what you have created in the life of the one you say you love. I've heard people say, "Love hurts." It does not mean Love inflicts hurt. It means when you feel

> **"Things covered don't heal."**

forced to let go of the one you love, you hurt. Oftentimes, we aren't able to feel another's pain simply because we are afraid of uncovering our own pain. You must understand, covered things never heal. We can mask the hurt all we want and act as if things are great with us, believing the problem lies only within our companion. But the truth remains, hurting people hurt people. I must be willing to look deep within and conquer my pain in order to help my spouse mend her pain. And nothing will help you feel another's pain like knowing you've got pain too.

Things covered don't heal. The more we suppress our own hurt, the more we are apt to suppress dealing with the hurt we've inflicted on others. I experienced what it felt like to have someone hurt me, and I had to deal with the fact that this person may never walk out the process of helping me through my healing process, but I have no control over them. This doesn't mean a person can't move on without the help of the person who hurt them, but it sure does make things a little bit easier, especially if the relationship is to continue.

Chapter 7

Taking Ownership

Most people know when they are wrong even if they don't acknowledge the wrong. Sometimes, we act like if we ignore the wrongs we've done it will be invisible. But, we must at some point acknowledge our ways and even go a step further to actually take ownership of what we've done wrong.

> **There's a difference in knowing you're wrong and taking ownership of the wrong.**

There's a difference in knowing you're wrong and taking ownership of the wrong. When we take ownership of something, we take responsibility for it. I remember when we purchased our first house, it was exciting to know I owned a house I was paying for with my own money. The house was in my name and it felt great. However, when they handed me the keys and I started moving in to this place I'd purchased, I thought of all the responsibilities that came with ownership. There were tons of yard work that had to be done because the previous owner thought they had a green thumb and had created a mess in the back. Parts of the house needed insulating and the basement needed to be finished, carpet needed to be laid. I found myself doing things I'd never done before, but the home was mine and I was faced with the challenge of making it better.

Once you gain ownership of something, the burden or joy of responsibility is all yours. Much like owning my first home, I realized owning the wrongs I'd done required me to embrace the responsibility of cleaning up and making things better. I had to clean up and make the situation with my wife better. There were things that had been planted that required me to do some pulling up and tearing down. The difference between the house and my marriage was I had planted the things in my marriage that needed to be dug up. Some of the things planted in the yard required me to seek help. I couldn't handle it all on my own. I eventually ended up seeking the help of God first, then the help of professionals, spiritual advisors or counselors. There's no shame in

> *Once you gain ownership of something, the burden or joy of responsibility is all yours.*

getting help. Seeking help is a clear sign that you've at least begun to realize this is your baby, and you've got to be about fixing it with the help of God.

Without counsel purposes are disappointed: but in the multitude of counsellors they are established (Proverbs 15:22).

Refuse good advice and watch your plans fail; take good counsel and watch them succeed (Amplified Bible).

- If men will not take time and pains to deliberate (carefully think or reflect), they are not likely to bring anything to pass.

My marriage was too important to me to allow my pride to get in the way of seeking the help I needed to fix it. I read books, listened to others speak on marriage and went to conferences for couples. Sometimes, when you don't know how to fix something you have to take self-help (DIY) courses. Do whatever works. Remember God will always meet you at the point where you can't do anything else. In other words, when you've done all you can, God won't leave you hanging. Your efforts won't go unnoticed. At the end of the day, you can't change anyone else, but you can absolutely change yourself. God will work through your change and begin to change your spouse's heart as He did my wife.

> **Remember, God will always meet you at the point you can't do anything else.**

Remember, God will always meet you at the point you can't do anything else. Go ahead and take ownership of the pain you may have inflicted or the confusion you may have caused or the burdens you may have given. Once you do, it will become much easier to face the one you've hurt with a true heart of remorse and compassion to mend their heart. Your spouse has to truly know and feel the sincerity of you owning up to the things you've done beyond another, "I'm sorry, I won't do it again" song and dance. Been there done that and yes, I have the t-shirt.

Chapter 8

Commit to Fight

It's so much easier to give up, throw in the towel and quit. But I've always been told anything worth having is worth fighting for. I don't know who originally coined the phrase, but its dead on. I must admit I wasn't the one to start a lot of fights back in my younger days, but I do remember the day of my fighting back days. There was a bully, bigger than most of the kids, in fifth grade. He had a habit of picking on much smaller kids. I wasn't big at all, and my dad was a man

> **Anything worth having is worth fighting for!**

who believed in getting what he paid for. Once in a while, he would take me to the barber with him to get a "Fair Daddy" haircut. This meant you got your head shaven. Fair to my daddy but not so fair to me. When I returned to school after having my hair cut, the bully had a tendency of slapping my head. He'd done it a few times before. However, this particular time, I'd had enough. I decided if he slapped me, it was going to be on. The bully came behind me in the hallway and sure enough, he did it again. POW! In a loud angry voice, I said, "That's it!" I commenced to give him a few blows he didn't expect, and we struggled on the floor. Ultimately, he got the best of me, but I fought back. To my surprise, I didn't have to deal with him anymore. Problem solved.

There comes a time when you've had enough of not enjoying your relationship. You have to determine you're going to get in the fight. Don't be defeated by your own pride or selfishness. Don't be defeated by disillusionment because your spouse doesn't acknowledge your attempts at doing better.

Anything worth having is worth fighting for! Sometimes when fighting, you'll be knocked down. But, don't stop fighting. Get back up before the count of ten and position yourself to continue the round. You're not fighting your spouse or even yourself. After you've dealt with yourself, you are now in an all-out attack of the devil. I believe destroying marriages is one of the devil's main targets for tearing down the family and community.

You can't expect to win a fight you're not participating in. Don't let another voice tell you it's no use, it's too late. It's over. No, you CAN do this. I determined to be with my wife until death do us part or until we transfer to heaven together. I had to fight those voices designed to give me a reason or an excuse to quit. Most of our reasons for giving up aren't reasons, they're excuses to why we shouldn't give our greatest efforts to salvage our marital relationship. I'm not saying there aren't true reasons for ending a relationship. I'm saying most of the time, we are too lazy or unwilling to make things work by first working on ourselves. I hear people say, "I am who I am and she or he has to accept me for who I am." News Flash! No, they don't and no, you don't. Nobody has to continue to accept anything less than what they believe is God's best for them. I know it is by the grace of God my wife and I are still together. Marriage is wonderful, but it's not necessarily easy.

> *When you're not engaged in the conversations with the intent to change, you miss a lot of what's being said.*

What are we fighting? We're not fighting our spouse! We're not fighting anything physical. We're fighting the pressures of our past actions or words. The hardest thing for some of us to do is let go of the past and move on to the next phase. Every time we think we've got it under control, our past raises up again. In order to defeat your enemy, you must know your enemy. You're in a battle against the situation trying to end your relationship.

Take out a piece of paper and write down all the things you've done to hurt your spouse. She or he has definitely told you what you've done, whether in a conversation or a heated

> **In order to make a change in our actions, we must replace those actions with new actions.**

argument. Even though my wife told me what I did over and over, I still couldn't repeat it back to her. Crazy, right? But, when you're not engaged in the conversation with the intent to change, you miss a lot of what's being said. After you've written these things down, you'll know what you did and said. And you'll know what they did and said. Now you have to fight not to repeat those things again with the help of God.

When you're not engaged in the conversations with the intent to change, you miss a lot of what's being said. In order to make a change in our actions, we must replace those actions with new actions. You have to determine the necessary opposite of the wrong you've done and do right.

For example, I had a habit of shutting down when I didn't want to respond to comments or questions my wife proposed to me. It wasn't that I was trying to be mean or ignore the question. This was my mechanism for not inflating the conversation to a shouting match. But, it was necessary that I exchange my shutting down with being more open even if I knew she wouldn't like my response. I developed the art of saying whatever I wanted to say in a way that was direct but not demeaning.

> *For every wrong there is a right, and you have to pursue the right to rid your wrong.*

For every wrong there is a right, and you have to pursue the right to rid your wrong. It will take the grace of God and our faith to save our marriage when it gets to the point where we feel there is no restoration. I'm reminded of the scripture, "For by grace are we saved through Faith." We were lost sinners not worthy of forgiveness, but by the grace (undeserving favor) of God and through our faith in Him, we are saved, forgiven and have a restored relationship with Him. We must trust while we are sincerely shifting our ways that God will touch the heart of our spouse. And we must have faith that our marriage relationship will be restored as our relationship with God was restored.

For every wrong there is a right, and you have to pursue the right to rid your wrong. It's always a fight to make a change. In order for change to take place, there has to be a change of mind and heart. *As a man thinketh in his heart so is he. (Proverbs 23:7).* Continuous thinking affects our heart. And based on this scripture, the mind and the heart work together to make us who we are. Once the heart and mind form a team effort to change you, change is inevitable. Our thoughts are developed in our mind, but they are carried out in our hearts. Until change happens in our heart, we will keep saying we're going to change and remain the same. I challenge you to do as I did, have a serious heart change. Decide to love your future with your wife in spite of your past. Say good-bye to all the voices telling you, you can't fix it and tell yourself you and God can do all things.

Chapter 9

Enjoy the Moments

When it seems things aren't perfect, there is no since of goodness, pleasantness, cheerfulness or happiness. We allow the bad to outweigh the good simply because the bad is screaming for our attention. It's like bad news over good news. Bad news travels so much faster. Though things aren't ideal, there are still times in your relationship that stimulate a moment of laughter or a smile to enjoy. It doesn't help the

> *We allow the bad to outweigh the good simply because the bad is screaming for our attention.*

situation to hang on so intensely to every bad thing you've experienced and miss those subtle moments you should be enjoying. At some point, you have to choose to forget the things that are behind and start reaching for the prize of forgetting and letting go. My wife and I had many great moments when we were going through our rough spell, but we both were missing them. So, I decided to major on the good moments. If she smiled at my jokes, I took it. When she gave in to a hug or touch from me, I maximized the moment. To do this, I had to become more attentive to her actions and not be passive about these moments.

> **If we don't have another burst of happiness, we can fall into an emotional down spin.**

We allow the bad to outweigh the good simply because the bad is screaming for our attention. I believe one of the missing pieces to a fulfilling relationship is the ability to enjoy moments of happiness. The truth is happiness isn't a constant. Happiness is a burst of great emotional moments. Think about it, at any moment something crazy could happen in your life and ruin your happiness for the moment. Then we wait for or create another happy moment. If we don't have another burst of happiness, we can fall into an emotional down spin. This is why we have to embrace each good moment as if it's our last. Whether it's a soft touch of the hand or a subtle compliment, it's time to release the past and embrace the future of what you are working for and believing God to do in your relationship. We often can't enjoy the moment because we still haven't broken the clutches of the hurt of our past. I once heard

> **Happiness is a burst of great emotional moments.**

Bishop Jakes say, "You can't expect someone else to make you happy. You have to create your own happiness." You can choose to stay angry or hurt as long as you want, or you can choose to let go and enjoy good moments and create an atmosphere to release the bad and embrace the good. But, you can't embrace both at the same time.

Happiness is a burst of great emotional moments. Though moments don't last forever, the decisions we make in a moment can ultimately change our life and if we let it, our marriage. Use these times to have productive conversations about your progress. Ask your spouse if there is anything you need to improve and then perhaps ask if they have noticed any improvements of your actions to better your relationship. Listen attentively and welcome feedback. Enjoy the moment. Hold them in your arms and let them know how much you appreciate them. My wife and I have learned how to enjoy the moments as we continue to work on having more consistent moments of happy times with each other. Prayer has been a huge part of noticing these precious moments. Sometimes, even bad moments can turn into sweet moments if you let them.

I specifically remember a time when we had a bad moment on what started out to be a great day. I had decided to take my wife shopping. We got into a heated dispute at the register, a total misunderstanding. When we got into the car, it was an all-out blow up. I pulled the car over and said, "Baby, this is clearly the work of the devil. We need to take a breath, grab hands and pray." I prayed a short but clear prayer asking God to help us both join sides against the enemy who was trying to ruin a perfectly wonderful day God has given us to enjoy each other. I asked Him to show my wife that my intentions were good. I apologized and asked God to please give her the heart to forgive me so we could continue to have the day He intended for us to enjoy. I ended the prayer and looked over at my wife whose face was full of tears. She apologized to me, we kissed and continued to enjoy a wonderful day. This was definitely one of those moments for us to enjoy. I honestly believe a marriage without God has to be the most difficult way to live. I'm not saying you can't be married without God, but since He instituted marriage why not turn to Him when things get out of sorts?

I'm reminded of the first time Adam and Eve enjoyed a moment together. The moment God presented Eve to him. Adam said, "This is bone of my bone and flesh of my flesh." I believe there was a great sense of excitement, celebration and enjoyment at this moment in his life. Probably like the first time you decided to make your spouse yours. If every moment in our relationship were like this, perhaps you wouldn't be reading this book and I wouldn't be writing it. Life is filled with all kinds of twist and turns, but it's up to us to reach out and grab all the great moments we can compile to make a happy life and do our best to rid ourselves of all the moments that cripple us from moving forward.

My wife and I aren't perfect by any sense of the word, but we have learned how to use the good moments to build our relationship to a point where we can be open with each other about everything. We try to maximize these moments to help us move to the next level of our relationship. We don't always know how to handle every moment but with each new moment, we go to school and we invite the teacher (God) and counselors, if needed, to help us. I pray God will help you see the enjoyable moments in your relationship as He has helped me.

Chapter 10

Count Your Blessings

Often, we look for something spectacular to be the blessings we count in our life. I encourage you to get a greater appreciation for the things God has given you and most importantly, the one He has blessed you to become one with. You are blessed to have this woman or man (women) in your life. I once heard it said we get excited that the grass always looks greener on the other side, but it turns out to be artificial turf. You have to know what you have is the real thing, and real grass requires watering and trimming. You don't get a perfect lawn by looking at it. You have to work on it. In counting your blessings, you will be required to show your appreciation by being patient with the process God is putting your spouse through as much as you're patient with your own personal process God is taking you through.

We have to be willing to not just forgive the past, but also forget it.

Brethren, I count not myself to have apprehended: but this one thing I do, forgetting those things which are behind, and reaching forth unto those things which are before, I press toward the mark for the prize of the high calling of God in Christ Jesus (Philippians 3:13-14).

I believe this scripture appeals to our marriage as much as it does our life. The past can indeed be a springboard for us to be driven to our best self, but it can also be the heaviest weight to us moving forward. As Paul the apostle states, if we are willing to forget the past or not allow the weight of the past to be at the forefront of our mind, we can then begin to focus on the prizes or opportunities that lie ahead. Life will always provide us with opportunities. The blessing is being prepared or able to recognize and embrace the opportunity without the barrier of the past. Some allow the opportunity to pass because we don't like the way the opportunity is packaged. With every opportunity, you can expect obstacles and hurdles to get over. But, I believe God doesn't give opportunity to those who aren't equipped with the capacity to leap over the hurdles and overcome the obstacles. If it was easy to obtain the prize, then Paul would not have said, "I press toward the goal for the prize." For the opportunity to rebuild our relationship in our marriage, we give God thanks.

You are blessed to have this opportunity to correct some mistakes. You can't change the past, but you can definitely build on the fact that you are still together. What was meant to break you, God wants to use to build you and your relationship. You may feel you've been knocked down, but I'm here to tell you, you haven't been counted out. Get up and reach for your blessing. Go back in your mind and pull out all those great times you've shared with one another. If you've been blessed to bring children into this world together, remind yourself they exist because God used you both to produce them. If you look deep enough, you will find blessings you've packed away.

Mending your marriage is like mending anything else. It requires certain tools and when we don't have the right tools for the job, we tend to improvise which can be counterproductive. Counting your blessings is one of the tools required for mending your marriage, and it cannot be improvised. Take the time to be grateful for this awesome person God has allowed you to share your life with. Gratitude is a powerful attribute.

My wife and I are now in an extreme place of gratitude for how God has helped us make it through difficult times together. We count it a blessing to be in this season of our marriage where we can now say all things worked together for our good. And though we aren't where we desire to be, we are well beyond where we were. We know it will always be tests to pass, but we have decided they won't be the same tests over and over again. We choose to pass the test and move on to the next and count ourselves blessed to have moved on to the next level of our relationship. I pray that you will do the same with your marriage. There's a blessing in every story. And there's a blessing in yours.

I bless your relationship and I ask God to breathe on your marriage today. Though it may have been as dead bones I believe that the breath of God can bring it to life again! I pray that each heart is mended to wholeness and completely healed to once again function in the full capacity as He has ordained. I declare and decree that new love will spring from the healing of old hurts. I pray that God will help you mend what you have broken and for it to be broken no longer.

God Bless Your Hearts.

Maurice Martin

About the Author

Maurice Martin was born in the small town of Ozark, Alabama currently residing in Kansas City, Missouri since 2001. He is the husband to his beautiful bride of thirty-two years, Jean Martin. He credits everything he has accomplished and will accomplish for the kingdom of God to her support and aid. He and his wife have a blended family of four children and ten grandchildren. His children and grandchildren fill his heart with joy just by being in their presence. He has served in many positions within the church, to include Deacon, Minister, Elder, Associate Pastor and Branch Pastor. Additionally, he served in many areas of ministry to include Men's Ministry, Premarital and Marriage Advisor, Director of Singles Ministry and Marriage Ministry. He believes pastoring is one of the most important forms of servanthood.

Maurice is also an author and keynote speaker. He has served in ministry for over thirty years, and has been teaching and preaching for over twenty-five years. He and his wife have served together in a Singles and Marriage Ministry for over 20 years helping to make relationships whole and secure through sound Kingdom centered principles. They both have a heart to see other relationships healthy and whole. Maurice is a lover of God, God's people and is called to effect change in the lives of individuals, couples and families. He stands on the Word of God as foundational truth and shares his personal marriage and life experiences with others helping guide them to a better relationship.

Maurice is available to speak at conferences and churches. You can connect with Maurice online at

Twitter:
MMartinMinistry

Facebook:
@mauricemartinministries

Instagram:
mauricemartinministries

Website:
mendingmarriedhearts.com

Email:
Maurice@mendingmarriedhearts.com

www.ingramcontent.com/pod-product-compliance
Lightning Source LLC
Chambersburg PA
CBHW052200090426
42741CB00010B/2350